100 FACTS ABOUT CATS

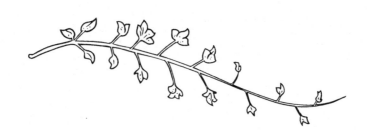

Welcome to a purrfectly captivating journey into the enchanting realm of our feline companions. In the pages that follow, we embark on a whisker-twitching exploration of the curious, the charming, and the utterly fascinating world of cats.

As we uncover 100 delightful facts, prepare to be whisked away into the mysterious corners of a cat's universe—from the ancient legends that celebrate their grace to the quirky behaviors that make them our most enigmatic friends.

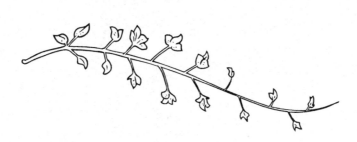

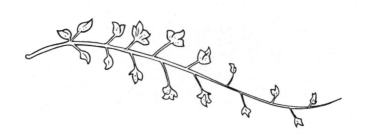

Whether you're a seasoned cat enthusiast or a curious reader eager to learn more about these captivating creatures, this book is a celebration of all things feline. We'll dive into the evolution of their species, unravel the secrets behind their purrs, and decode the unique language that exists between cats and their devoted human companions.

So, dear reader, grab a cozy blanket, find a sunny spot by the window, and let's embark on a journey where every fact is a step further into the delightful world of cats. Here's to whiskers, wonder, and a hundred feline tales!

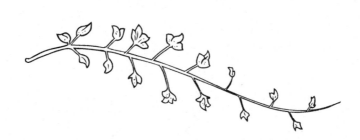

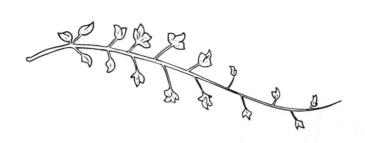

Before we dive into the intriguing world of cat facts, we extend our heartfelt gratitude to those who make this journey possible:
To the cats, both regal and mischievous, who inspire awe and affection with every purr and every play.To the cat enthusiasts, caregivers, and guardians, whose love and devotion create a world where feline wonders thrive.
To the researchers, veterinarians, and animal behaviorists who continue to unravel the mysteries of our furry companions.
To the artists and photographers whose images grace these pages, capturing the essence of cats in all their glory.

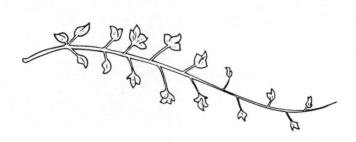

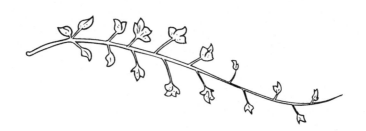

Copyright Information

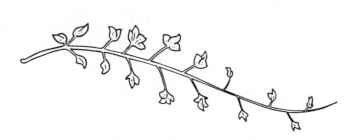

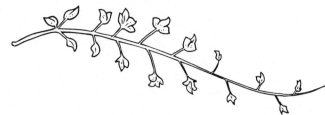

Ancient Egyptian Deities: Cats were highly revered in ancient Egypt and were associated with the goddess Bastet, the goddess of home, fertility, and protection.

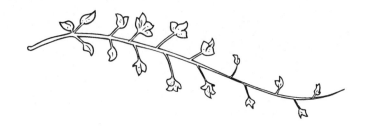

First Domesticated Animals: Cats were likely one of the first animals to be domesticated by humans, with evidence dating back over 9,000 years.

Purring Therapy: The sound frequency of a cat's purring is known to have therapeutic effects, promoting healing and reducing stress in humans.

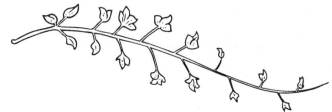

Flexible Spines: Cats have highly flexible spines, allowing them to twist their bodies mid-air and always land on their feet. This ability is known as the "righting reflex."

Unique Nose Prints:

Similar to human fingerprints, each cat's nose has a unique pattern of bumps and ridges, making their nose prints distinctive.

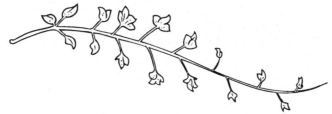

Eyes in the Dark: Cats can see in almost total darkness due to their highly sensitive rod cells in the retina.

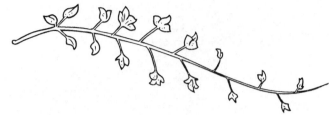

Whisker Fatigue:

Whiskers are highly sensitive touch receptors. If a cat's whiskers touch something, it can cause "whisker fatigue," making the cat uncomfortable.

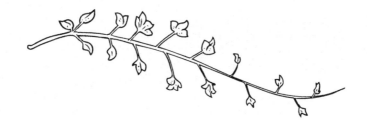

Language Variety: Cats have a wide range of vocalizations, including meows, purrs, chirps, and hisses, each serving different communication purposes.

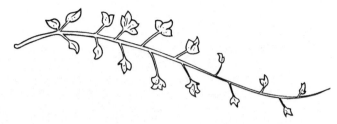

Mousing Diplomacy: In the 10th century, Vikings are said to have brought cats on their ships to control the rodent population, spreading the feline population across Europe.

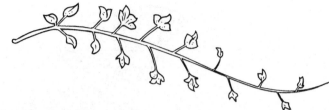

Famous Artists' Companions: Artists like Pablo Picasso, Mark Twain, and Ernest Hemingway were known to have had a deep affinity for cats, often featuring them in their works.

Herding Cats?: The phrase "herding cats" is often used to describe a challenging task, as cats are notoriously independent and may not follow orders.

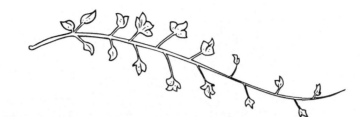

Cat's Sixth Sense: Cats are known to sense earthquakes before they occur, thanks to their highly developed sense of hearing and ability to detect vibrations.

Sleeping Masters: On average, cats sleep for 12-16 hours a day, conserving energy for their nocturnal hunting instincts.

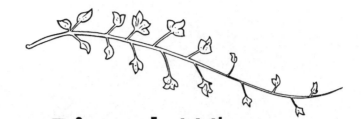

Kneading Ritual: When cats knead with their paws on a soft surface, it's a behavior learned from kittenhood, associated with the comforting feeling of nursing.

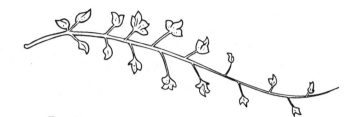

Cat-astrophic Nap: A cat named Félix Faure, residing in the Élysée Palace in France, triggered an international incident in 1897 when he napped on the bed of the President of France, Félix Faure.

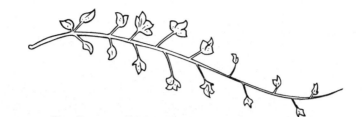

Cat-astrophic Nap: A cat named Félix Faure, residing in the Élysée Palace in France, triggered an international incident in 1897 when he napped on the bed of the President of France, Félix Faure.

Tallest Domestic Cat:

Arcturus Aldebaran Powers holds the Guinness World Record for the tallest domestic cat, measuring at 19.05 inches.

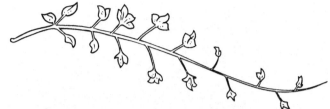

Longest Domestic Cat

Tail: Stewie, a Maine Coon, holds the record for the longest domestic cat tail, measuring an impressive 16.34 inches.

Cat Burglar: A cat named Dusty became known as a "cat burglar" in San Mateo, California, stealing items from neighbors' homes and bringing them to his owner.

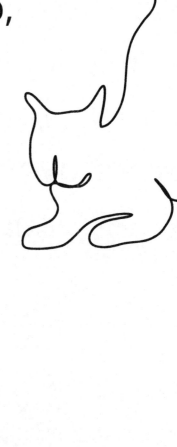

Oldest Recorded Pet Cat:

The oldest known pet cat was discovered on the Mediterranean island of Cyprus, buried with its owner over 9,000 years ago.

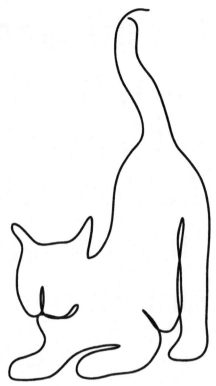

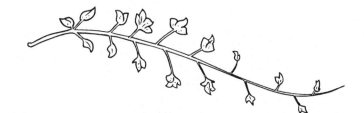

Cat's Reflex Speed: Cats have a rapid reflex that allows them to twist their bodies and land on their feet if they fall, thanks to their flexible spine and lack of a collarbone.

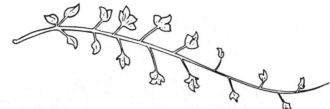

Cats Understand Their Names: Research has shown that cats can distinguish their names from other words, even though they may choose to ignore them.

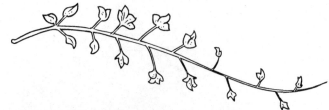

Famous Internet Cats:

Grumpy Cat, Lil Bub, and Keyboard Cat are among the most famous cats on the internet, with millions of followers.

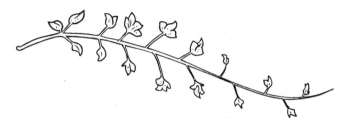

Cat Café Trend: The first cat café, where customers can enjoy beverages and interact with resident cats, opened in Taipei, Taiwan, in 1998, sparking a global trend.

Feline Weather Predictors: Cats are believed to be able to predict changes in the weather, particularly sensing earthquakes or storms.

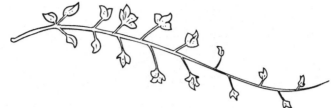

Nyan Cat Meme: The Nyan Cat, a popular internet meme, features a cat with a Pop-Tart body flying through space, accompanied by a catchy tune.

Maternal Surrogacy: In 2015, a cat named Rademenesa became a nurse at a Polish animal shelter, comforting and caring for sick animals.

Ancient Cat Burials: Cats were often buried with their owners in ancient Egyptian tombs, symbolizing protection in the afterlife.

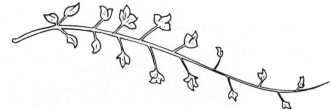

Cat's Navigation Skills:

Cats have an incredible ability to find their way home, even when moved to a new location.

Cat's Unique Grooming Pattern: Cats groom themselves in a specific pattern, starting with licking their lips, then front legs, followed by their face, ears, and finishing with the back.

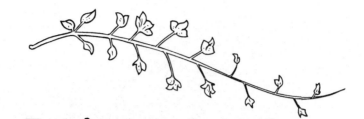

Whisker Fatigue: A cat's whiskers are highly sensitive and can detect changes in air currents, allowing them to navigate in the dark.

Feline "Kiss": Slow blinking at a cat is considered a sign of trust and affection, often referred to as a "cat kiss."

Cat Allergies:

Approximately 10% of the human population is allergic to cats, with reactions triggered by proteins in their saliva, urine, and dander.

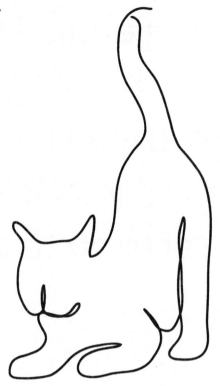

Cats Have a Dominant Paw:
Like humans being right or left-handed, cats can have a preference for using one paw over the other.

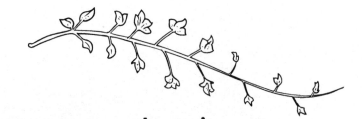

Lap Warmer: Ancient mariners believed that cats brought good luck to ships and protected them from evil spirits.

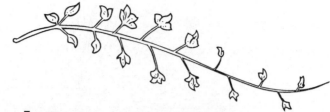

Cats and Pregnancy:

Pregnant women are advised to avoid cleaning litter boxes due to the risk of toxoplasmosis, a parasite found in cat feces.

Cat's Grooming Ritual:

Grooming not only keeps a cat's fur clean but also helps distribute natural oils, promoting healthy skin.

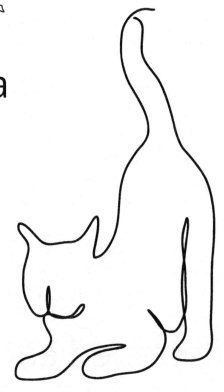

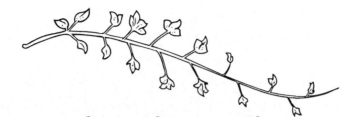

Ear Communication: The direction a cat's ears are facing can indicate their mood. Forward-facing ears signal curiosity or friendliness, while flattened ears indicate fear or aggression.

Cat's Nose Prints: Each cat has a unique nose print, similar to a human fingerprint.

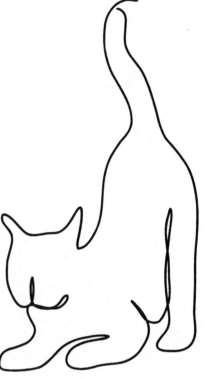

Tallest Cat Stature: The Savannah cat holds the record for the tallest domestic cat breed, standing at up to 19 inches at the shoulder.

Cat's Night Vision: Cats can see in light levels six times lower than what a human needs, making them excellent hunters during the night.

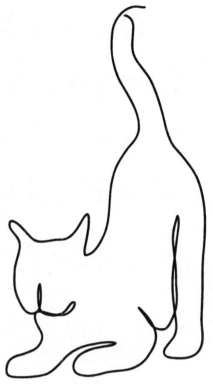

Oldest Known Pet Cemetery: The world's oldest pet cemetery was discovered in Egypt, dating back over 2,000 years.

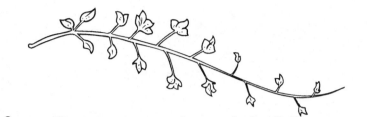

First Cat in Space: In 1963, France sent the first cat, named Félix, into space to study the effects of weightlessness on living organisms.

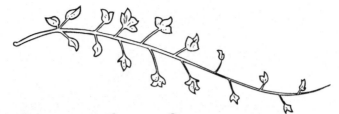

Cat Olympics: The first Cat Olympics, known as the "Feline Agility Competition," took place in 2012 during the Meet the Breeds event in New York City.

Record for the Most Kittens: A cat named Dusty holds the record for the most kittens born in her lifetime, a staggering 420 kittens.

Cat's Incredible Jumping Ability: Cats can jump up to five times their own height in a single leap.

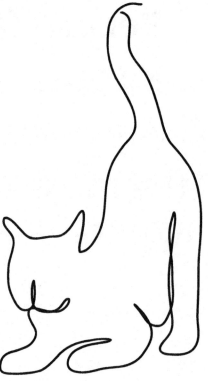

Cat-astrophic Invention:

In 1871, a patent was issued for a cat-shaped brush designed to apply ink to printing plates, known as the "cat printer."

Catnip Response: Catnip contains a compound called nepetalactone that triggers a temporary behavioral response in cats, making them roll, flip, and exhibit playful behavior.

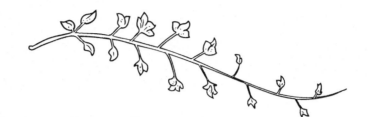

Ancient Cat Sculptures: In ancient Egypt, statues of cats were believed to bring good luck and protect the home from evil spirits.

Cat's Unique Meow: Cats develop unique meows to communicate with their owners, adapting their vocalizations based on their needs and desires.

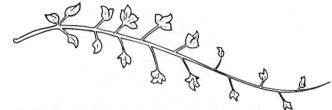

Famous Fictional Cats:

Cheshire Cat from "Alice in Wonderland," Garfield, and Puss in Boots are iconic fictional cats that have left a mark on literature and popular culture.

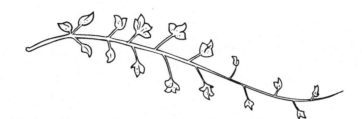

Cat Café Popularity: The first cat café in the United States, "Cat Town Café," opened in Oakland, California, in 2014, inspiring a trend across the country.

Cat's Healing Purr: The vibrations created by a cat's purring are believed to have healing properties, promoting bone density and reducing pain and inflammation.

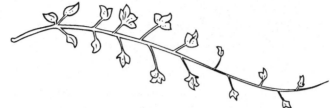

Cat's Territory Marking:

Cats mark their territory by rubbing their scent glands located on their cheeks against objects, people, or other cats.

Largest Cat Painting: A painting titled "My Wife's Lovers" holds the record for the largest cat painting, featuring 42 cats and measuring 6 feet by 8.5 feet.

Cat Naps and REM Sleep:

Cats experience REM (rapid eye movement) sleep, suggesting they dream just like humans during their naps.

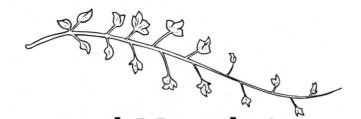

Cat's Ears and Mood: A cat with its ears straight up indicates that it is happy and content, while flattened ears signal fear or aggression.

Cat's Tail Communication:

A cat's tail position can convey its mood—upright tails signal happiness, while a puffed-up tail indicates fear or agitation.

First Commercial Cat Food: Spratt's, a British electrician, invented the first commercial cat food in the late 1800s, called "Spratt's Patent Cat Food."

Cat's Cultural Significance: Cats are featured prominently in folklore, mythology, and superstitions around the world, symbolizing various traits from mystery to luck.

Cat's Superior Night Vision: Cats have a structure called the tapetum lucidum in their eyes, which enhances their night vision by reflecting light back through their retinas.

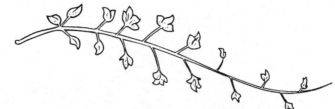

Cat and Human Bonding:

Mutual grooming, where cats and humans groom each other, is considered a bonding activity and a sign of affection.

First Cat Show: The world's first official cat show took place in London in 1871, featuring over 170 cats.

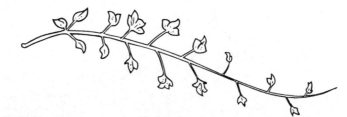

Cats and Water: Most cats dislike water, which can be traced back to their ancestors in arid environments where water was scarce.

Cat's Rapid Heartbeat: A cat's heart beats nearly twice as fast as a human's, with an average of 140-220 beats per minute.

First Cat Movie Star: The first cat to become a movie star was Pepper, who appeared in the 1910 film "Rescued by Rover."

Cat and Owl Friendship:

In 2015, an unusual friendship between a cat named Fum and an owl named Gebra went viral, showcasing their playful interactions.

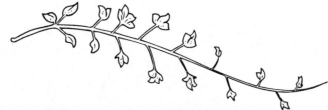

Oldest Known Cat Drawing: A 9,000-year-old drawing of a cat was discovered on the Mediterranean island of Cyprus.

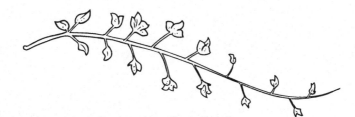

Cat and Rat Friendship: In a Belgian zoo, a stray cat named Remy befriended a giant rat named Ratatouille, showcasing the unusual bonds animals can form.

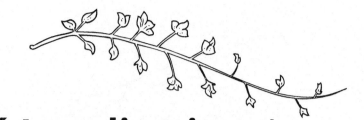

Cat Café Legalization: In 2018, California became the first state to legalize the operation of cat cafés, allowing customers to enjoy the company of cats while sipping coffee.

Cat and Lizard Friendship: A cat named Bagel formed an unlikely friendship with a bearded dragon named Rango, showcasing the diverse bonds animals can create.

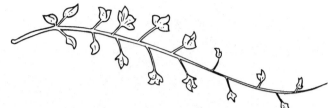

Cat's Unique Grooming Pattern: Cats groom themselves in a specific pattern, starting with licking their lips, then front legs, followed by their face, ears, and finishing with the back.

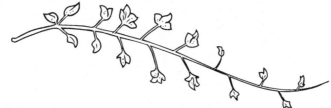

Cat's Purring Healing Properties: The frequency of a cat's purring is believed to have healing properties, promoting bone density, reducing pain, and aiding in tissue repair.

Cats and National Geographic: National Geographic has featured cats in various documentaries, highlighting their behaviors, habitats, and unique adaptations.

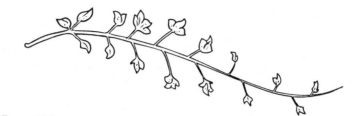

Cat with Two Faces: In 2019, a rare two-faced cat named Narnia gained international attention for its unique appearance, featuring a perfectly split face with two different eye colors.

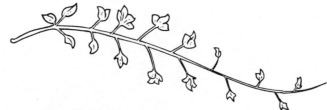

Cat's Unique Communication Methods: Cats communicate through various means, including vocalizations, body language, and scent marking.

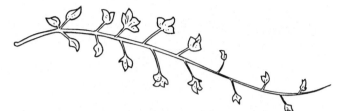

Cat Naps and REM Sleep:

Cats experience REM (rapid eye movement) sleep, suggesting they dream just like humans during their naps.

Cat's Ears and Mood: A cat with its ears straight up indicates that it is happy and content, while flattened ears signal fear or aggression.

Cat's Tail Communication: A cat's tail position can convey its mood—upright tails signal happiness, while a puffed-up tail indicates fear or agitation.

First Commercial Cat Food: Spratt's, a British electrician, invented the first commercial cat food in the late 1800s, called "Spratt's Patent Cat Food."

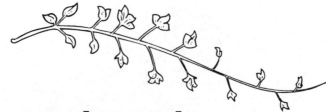

Cat's Cultural Significance: Cats are featured prominently in folklore, mythology, and superstitions around the world, symbolizing various traits from mystery to luck.

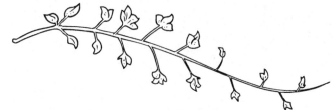

Cat's Superior Night Vision: Cats have a structure called the tapetum lucidum in their eyes, which enhances their night vision by reflecting light back through their retinas.

Cat and Human Bonding:
Mutual grooming, where cats and humans groom each other, is considered a bonding activity and a sign of affection.

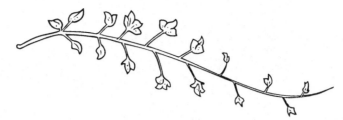

First Cat Show: The world's first official cat show took place in London in 1871, featuring over 170 cats.

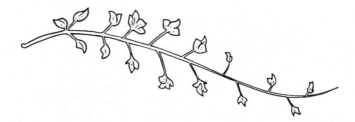

Cats and Water: Most cats dislike water, which can be traced back to their ancestors in arid environments where water was scarce.

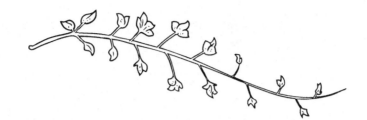

Cat's Rapid Heartbeat: A cat's heart beats nearly twice as fast as a human's, with an average of 140-220 beats per minute.

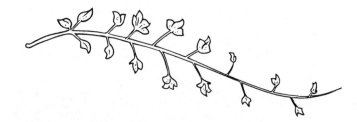

First Cat Movie Star: The first cat to become a movie star was Pepper, who appeared in the 1910 film "Rescued by Rover."

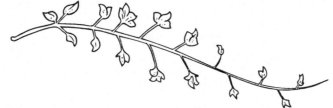

Cat and Owl Friendship:

In 2015, an unusual friendship between a cat named Fum and an owl named Gebra went viral, showcasing their playful interactions.

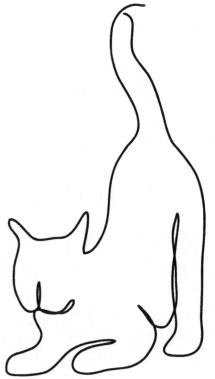

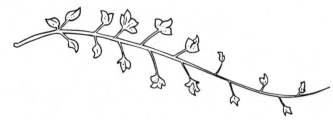

Isle of Man Cat: The Manx cat, originating from the Isle of Man, is known for its taillessness or short tails.

Japanese Bobtail and Lucky Charms: The Japanese Bobtail, known for its distinctive short tail, is often associated with good luck in Japanese culture.

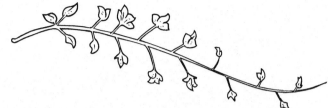

Lil Bub: Lil Bub, a cat with unique physical traits due to genetic mutations, gained popularity on the internet and became an advocate for special-needs animals before passing away in 2019.

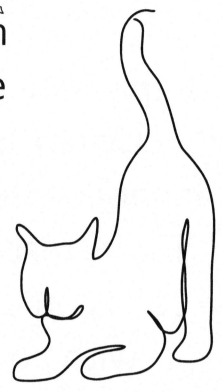

Famous Cat Artists: Cats have been featured in art by renowned artists, such as Édouard Manet's "Olympia" and Pablo Picasso's "Cat Catching a Bird."

Internet Cat Videos: Cats became internet sensations through platforms like YouTube, with viral videos of cats exhibiting quirky behaviors gaining millions of views.

Cat Café Trend: The first cat café, where patrons can enjoy the company of resident cats, opened in Taipei, Taiwan, in 1998. The trend has since spread globally.

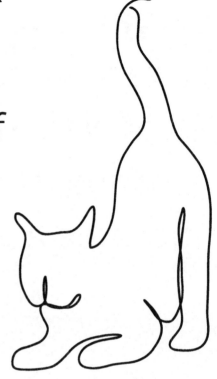

Nyan Cat: Nyan Cat, an internet meme featuring a cat with a Pop-Tart body flying through space, became a viral sensation in 2011.

Garfield: Created by Jim Davis, Garfield is a lasagna-loving cat known for his sarcastic humor. The comic strip debuted in 1978.

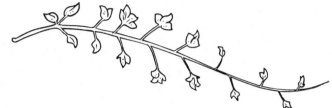

Hello Kitty: Created by Sanrio in 1974, Hello Kitty is a globally recognized character, symbolizing kawaii (cuteness) in Japanese pop culture.

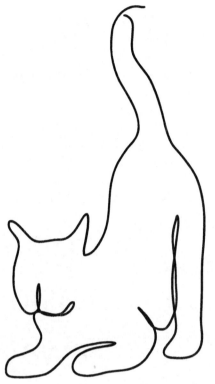

Grumpy Cat: Grumpy Cat, whose real name was Tardar Sauce, gained worldwide fame due to her distinctive facial expression. She passed away in 2019.

Famous Literary Cats:
Cats have appeared in numerous literary works, such as Puss in Boots (Charles Perrault) and the Cheshire Cat (Lewis Carroll's "Alice's Adventures in Wonderland").

Tuxedo Cats in Popular Culture: Tuxedo cats, with their distinctive black and white coat resembling a formal suit, have been popular in literature and film, including the character Sylvester from Looney Tunes.

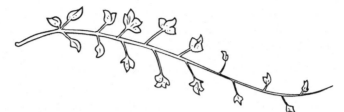

Cat Fanciers' Association (CFA): Founded in 1906, the CFA is the world's largest registry of pedigreed cats and a prominent organization in the cat fancy community.

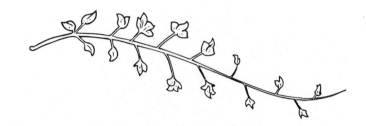

First Cat Show: The world's first cat show took place in London in 1871, organized by Harrison Weir, a British artist and cat enthusiast.

The Black Plague and Cats: Ironically, the persecution of cats during the Black Plague may have worsened the spread of the disease, as cats could have helped control the rat population carrying the plague.

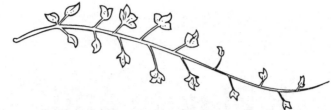

Domestication in the Fertile Crescent: Cats likely became domesticated around 7500 BCE in the Fertile Crescent, where they played a role in controlling rodent populations around early agricultural settlements.

Ancient Egyptian Reverence: Cats were highly revered in ancient Egypt, with the goddess Bastet depicted as a lioness or a woman with the head of a lioness, symbolizing protection.

Cats and Wildlife Conservation: Cats can have significant impacts on local wildlife, especially when allowed to roam freely outdoors. Responsible pet ownership, including keeping cats indoors or supervised in enclosed spaces, helps protect both domestic and wild animals.

Insect Huntress: Cats are excellent hunters of insects. While they may not form friendships with bugs, their instinct to catch and play with them is a natural behavior that many cat owners observe.

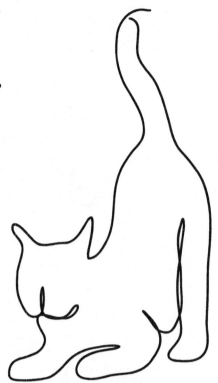

Cats and Reptiles: Cats may share homes with reptiles like turtles or snakes. Careful supervision is necessary to prevent any harm, and providing separate spaces for each pet is often recommended.

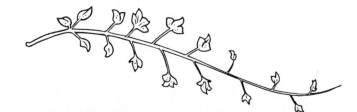

Felines and Fish: Some cats are intrigued by fish, whether in home aquariums or outdoor ponds. While they may watch fish with fascination, it's essential to ensure the safety of both the cat and the aquatic creatures.

Cats and Rodents: While cats are natural predators of rodents, they can also form relationships with pet rodents, such as hamsters and guinea pigs. Proper supervision is crucial to ensure everyone's safety.

Feline Equine Bonds: Cats are known to form connections with horses. Whether in barns or on farms, cats often share spaces with horses, offering companionship and sometimes helping control rodent populations.

Cats and Birds: While cats are natural hunters, some cats develop unique relationships with birds. In certain cases, they may peacefully coexist, even sharing spaces within the same household.

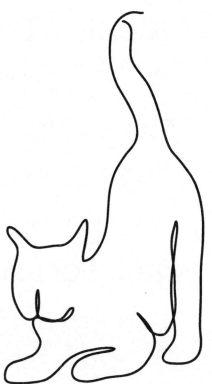

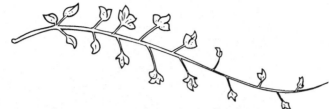

Canine Companionship:

Despite popular stereotypes, many cats and dogs coexist harmoniously. With proper introductions and socialization, cats can form strong bonds with dogs, showcasing the potential for interspecies friendships.

Cats and Canaries: In history, some households kept both cats and canaries as pets. While the canary's song might capture the cat's attention, careful introduction and supervision were necessary to prevent any harm to the bird.

Aquatic Adventures:

Certain cat breeds, like the Turkish Van, are known for their affinity for water. They may form playful connections with aquatic animals, exploring ponds or even joining their human companions during fishing trips.

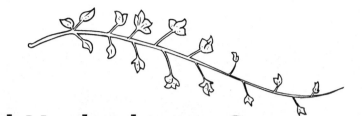

Cats and Hedgehogs: Some cats show interest in hedgehogs. While caution is essential to prevent any harm to the spiky creatures, supervised interactions may reveal unexpected friendships between felines and hedgehogs.

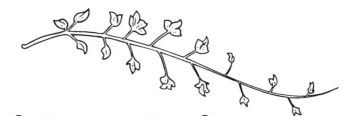

Cats and Cows: On farms, cats often forge bonds with cows. Cats may find warmth and companionship in the barns and fields where cows graze, fostering unique interspecies connections.

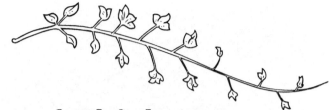

Cats and Chickens:

Surprisingly, cats and chickens can share spaces peacefully. In rural settings, cats often coexist with chickens, providing pest control services while maintaining a harmonious relationship.

Orphaned Wildlife Bonds:

Some domestic cats have formed bonds with orphaned wild animals. Instances of cats adopting abandoned squirrels, raccoons, or even small deer have been documented, showcasing their nurturing nature.

Cross-Species Adoption: In rare cases, mother cats have been known to adopt and nurse the offspring of other species, such as puppies or even baby rabbits, demonstrating a nurturing instinct beyond their own kind.

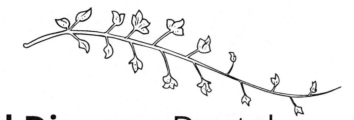

Dental Disease: Dental problems are common in cats, ranging from gingivitis to tooth decay. Regular dental care, including brushing, can help prevent these issues.

Hyperthyroidism: This condition results from an overactive thyroid gland, commonly seen in older cats. Symptoms include weight loss, increased appetite, and hyperactivity.

Chronic Kidney Disease (CKD): Older cats are prone to CKD, which affects the kidneys' ability to function properly. Early detection and management are essential for a cat's quality of life.

Feline Diabetes Mellitus:

Cats can develop diabetes, especially those that are overweight. Symptoms include increased thirst, frequent urination, and weight loss.

Urinary Tract Infections (UTIs): Cats, especially males, can suffer from UTIs. Common symptoms include frequent urination, straining, and blood in the urine.

Feline Panleukopenia (Feline Distemper): This highly contagious viral disease affects a cat's blood cells and intestines. Vaccination is crucial to prevent this potentially fatal illness.

Feline Immunodeficiency Virus (FIV): Similar to HIV in humans, FIV weakens a cat's immune system. It's often transmitted through bites, and outdoor male cats are more prone to infection.

Feline Leukemia Virus (FeLV): FeLV is a contagious virus that weakens a cat's immune system, making it susceptible to other infections. It is spread through close contact, and outdoor cats are at higher risk.

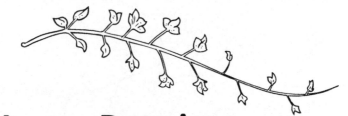

Feline Upper Respiratory Infections (URI): URIs are common in cats, especially those in crowded environments like shelters. Symptoms include sneezing, nasal discharge, and conjunctivitis.

Coccidia: Coccidia are microscopic parasites that can cause diarrhea in cats, especially in kittens. Proper hygiene and sanitation are crucial in preventing the spread of coccidiosis.

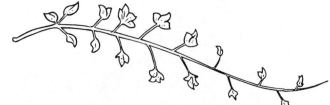

Sarcoptic Mange: Sarcoptic mange, caused by Sarcoptes scabiei mites, results in intense itching, hair loss, and skin irritation. It is highly contagious among animals.

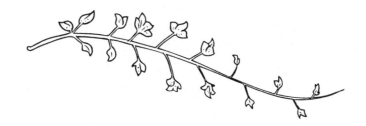

Demodex Mites: Demodex mites can cause skin issues in cats, leading to hair loss and skin inflammation. While present on most cats, issues arise when the mites proliferate.

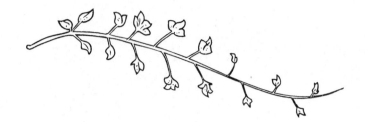

Cheyletiella Mites (Walking Dandruff): These mites infest a cat's skin, causing itching and a distinctive appearance of moving dandruff. They are contagious among pets.

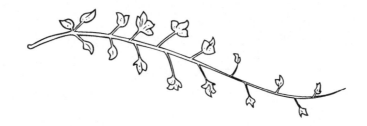

Toxoplasma gondii: Cats can host the Toxoplasma gondii parasite, which is especially concerning for pregnant women due to potential transmission risks. Proper hygiene and care can minimize the risk.

Heartworms: While more commonly associated with dogs, cats can also contract heartworm disease, a potentially fatal condition transmitted through mosquito bites.

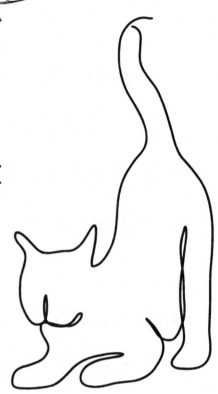

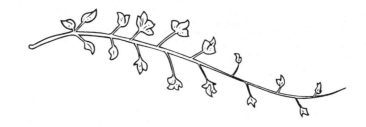

Intestinal Worms:

Common intestinal parasites in cats include roundworms, tapeworms, hookworms, and whipworms. Infestations can lead to digestive issues, weight loss, and lethargy.

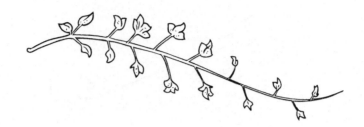

Ear Mites: Ear mites are tiny parasites that infest a cat's ears, leading to discomfort, itching, and possible ear infections. They are highly contagious and often seen in kittens.

Ticks: Ticks are blood-sucking parasites that can transmit various diseases, such as Lyme disease and anaplasmosis, to cats. Regular tick checks and preventive measures are crucial.

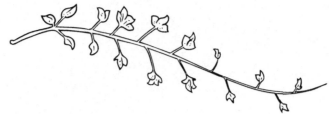

Fleas: Fleas are common external parasites that can infest cats, causing itching, skin irritation, and even transmitting diseases like Bartonella (cat scratch fever).

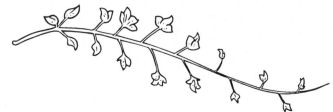

Obesity Impact: Obesity is a significant health risk for cats and can reduce their lifespan. Maintaining a healthy weight through proper diet and exercise is crucial.

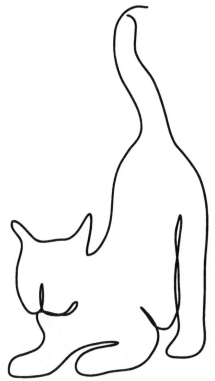

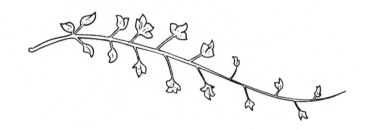

Physical Activity: Regular exercise is beneficial for a cat's physical and mental well-being. Engaging in play and providing opportunities for physical activity can contribute to a healthier and longer life.

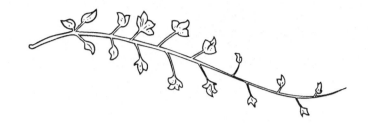

Veterinary Care: Regular veterinary check-ups, vaccinations, and preventive care can contribute to a longer and healthier life for a cat. Early detection and treatment of health issues are crucial.

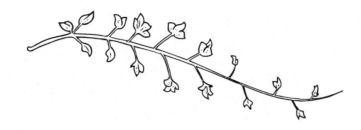

Spaying/Neutering Impact: Spayed and neutered cats often live longer than intact cats. Spaying and neutering reduce the risk of certain health issues and behaviors that may put a cat at risk.

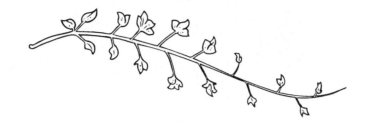

Breed Influence: Different cat breeds may have varying lifespans. Some breeds, like the Siamese and Ragdoll, are known for living into their late teens or early twenties, while others, like the Manx, may have a shorter lifespan.

Chirps and Trills: Cats may produce chirping or trilling sounds, often observed when they are excited, curious, or attempting to get the attention of their owners. These sounds are typically of moderate volume.

Behavioral Responses:

Cats may be more aloof and independent in their responses to stimuli, while dogs are often more expressive and may react with excitement, fear, or aggression based on their social and protective instincts.

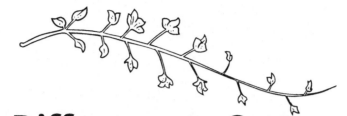

Dietary Differences: Cats are obligate carnivores, meaning they require a diet primarily composed of meat. Dogs are omnivores and can have a more varied diet that may include both animal and plant-based ingredients.

Territorial Behavior: Cats are territorial animals and may mark their territory with scent glands on their face, paws, and tail. Dogs can also exhibit territorial behavior but are generally more adaptable to shared spaces.

Grooming Habits: Cats are meticulous groomers and clean themselves regularly. They have barbed tongues that aid in cleaning their fur. Dogs may need more frequent baths, and some breeds with longer fur may require regular grooming.

Training Approaches: Dogs are generally easier to train than cats. They respond well to commands, positive reinforcement, and consistent training. Cats, while trainable to some extent, are more independent and may not always follow commands.

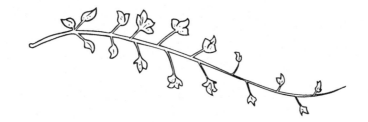

Communication Styles: Dogs are generally more expressive and vocal in their communication. They use barking, whining, and body language to convey their feelings. Cats communicate more subtly, using a range of vocalizations like meowing, purring, and hissing, as well as body language like tail movements and ear positions.

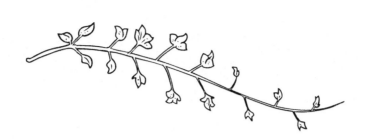

Thank you for Exploring "100 Facts About Cats"

As we turn the final page of this feline-filled journey, we want to extend a heartfelt thank you for joining us on this whisker-twisting adventure through the captivating world of cats.

Whether you're a dedicated cat lover, a curious explorer of the animal kingdom, or someone simply seeking a delightful read, we hope you've enjoyed uncovering the many facets of our mysterious and endearing feline friends.

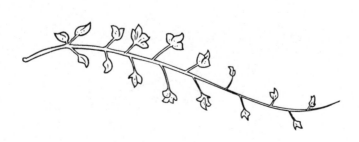

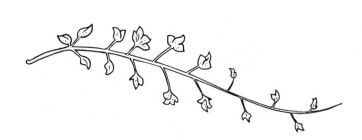

Cats, with their grace, humor, and unpredictable antics, have a way of leaving pawprints on our hearts. We hope these 100 facts have deepened your appreciation for the incredible diversity and charm that cats bring into our lives.

As you close this book, may you carry with you a newfound understanding of these enigmatic creatures. From their ancient history to their modern roles as companions, may the spirit of the cat continue to captivate your imagination.

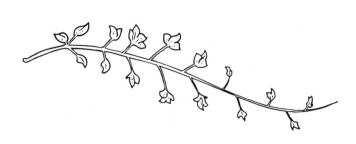

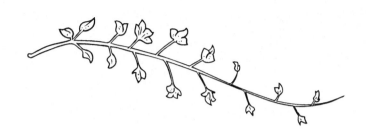

Thank you for being part of this journey into the fascinating universe of cats. Until our paths cross again, may your days be filled with purrs, soft fur, and the timeless allure of our feline friends.

Paws and whiskers,
John Hick

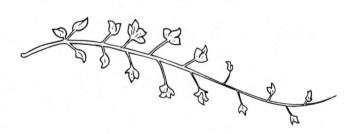

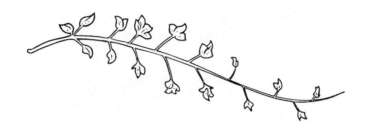

Thank you for being part of this journey into the fascinating universe of cats. Until our paths cross again, may your days be filled with purrs, soft fur, and the timeless allure of our feline friends.

Paws and whiskers,
John Hick

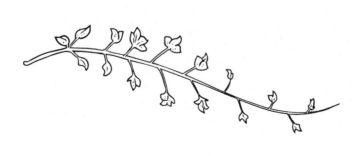